NOW THAT YOU
HAVE RECEIVED
Christ

Babatunde Akinfisoye

KEBABI
PUBLICATIONS

Published by Kebabi Publications

Text copyright © Babatunde Akinfisoye, 2011

First published May 2011 by First Call Publishing Ltd

Revised Edition 2016

ISBN 978-0-9926190-1-5

Cover design/text layout by Imaginovation

Edited by Kemisola Akinfisoye

Printed in UK by Kebabi Publications

CONTENTS

Acknowledgement

I am deeply grateful to my precious Heavenly Father, my Lord and Saviour Jesus Christ and the wonderful Holy Spirit. You delivered me from destruction and brought me into Your kingdom. Your investment in my life is immeasurable and I am eternally grateful.

I bless God for my beautiful family: my loving wife Kemisola, who has always stood by me and supported me in the ministry that God has given me, and our wonderful sons Ireoluwa and Anuoluwa – you are indeed God's goodness and mercy, and it is my prayer that you will both love and serve our Lord and Master all the days of your lives.

I thank God for my late parents, Mr Joseph Okunfulure and Mrs Mercy Modupe Akinfisoye who raised me. You were both amazing and I will always bless God for your lives. To my siblings: we went through a lot together, but I thank God for always showing Himself faithful in our lives. I couldn't have chosen a better family to come from. My sister, Yinka Olaiya, thank you for being a good example to us, and particularly for those scriptures you wrote in the Bible you gave to me many years ago (1 Timothy 4:15 and 2 Timothy 2:15), which have gone a long way in shaping my destiny.

I must mention my gratitude to the Lord for my late sister-in-law, Doyin, who is resting and enjoying her time with her father. It was through you that I met your sister, my wife Kemisola, and the entire family and I am thankful for the wonderful addition to my family.

I really appreciate the leadership of Jesus House, particularly my Pastor and father in the faith, Pastor Agu Irukwu – thank you for your wonderful leadership and support. Pastor Shola Adeaga, my wife and I can never forget your wise words and warm welcome to us when we came to Jesus House in June 2006. Pastor Bolanle Ojeh, thank you for being an amazing sister and Head of Department. Our testimony is that we have been richly blessed by both members and leaders alike. The idea of writing this book has been with me for well over 15 years but you have helped me make it a reality. God bless you.

First Call Publishing Limited, thanks for all your help and the excellent work you have done. The Lord will never forget your labour of love.

Foreword

Effective discipleship remains the missing ingredient in the development of believers in this age. Life events appear to move very fast and it is as if Christianity itself should be brought into the 'microwavable' products. Not so, declares the author. He argues that Christian growth is a process and discipleship is a necessary part of that process.

The author employs simple and easy-to-understand language to help the reader appreciate the necessity, both on the part of mature Christians and new believers, of embarking on a process of Christian maturity early in one's Christian walk. Using his personal conversion and growth experience, he elucidates the place that follow-up, fellowship, commitment to regular Bible study, prayer and mentoring played in his Christian faith development. He presents the ingredients necessary for a new believer to grow and remain steadfast in the faith in easy-to-follow steps.

This book will greatly help a new believer to understand what he can do to grow in his new-found faith. It is therefore a good resource for churches' discipleship ministries. Reading through the book was a blessing to me and I believe you too will find it useful in your walk with Christ.

Dr Daniel Akhazemea
Principal, Christ the Redeemer College

Introduction

These were more noble...

These were more noble than those in Thessalonica, in that they received the word with all readiness of mind, and searched the scriptures daily, whether those things were so. (Acts 17:11)

For every believer, the difference between living a victorious and successful Christian life and that of mediocrity is dependent majorly on the steps taken after accepting Jesus Christ as Lord and Saviour.

Some are fortunate to have accepted Christ in congregations or assemblies where there are excellent follow-up strategies for converts and are taught the rudiments of the Christian faith. Others are not so fortunate and are left alone to fend for themselves, resulting in many falling by the wayside. Better still, some take the responsibility for growth as a personal challenge, studying God's Word prayerfully and walking in line with His purpose and counsel.

As a young Christian, I was fortunate to have obtained good Christian counsel and follow-up from fellow students who were members of the Christian Union on campus, and who had been in the Christian race before me. I also had the opportunity to obtain counsel from older Christians – members of the Scripture Union

Fellowship I attended after my university education.

While these people did their best to guide me in the right direction, there were moments when I couldn't obtain satisfactory answers to some of the questions I had as a young Christian, and at such times I had to seek answers directly from the Lord through a prayerful study of His Word and reliance on the Holy Spirit.

While this book does not promise to answer all the questions a new Christian will have, it does seek to provide a basic guideline on steps that a new Christian should take immediately after accepting Jesus Christ as Lord and Saviour. These steps will help ensure success and victory in any Christian's life.

Particular emphasis is laid on the study of God's Word, as this is a key determinant of whether one becomes a noble Christian or a mediocre one. This can be clearly seen in our opening scripture, which describes the Christians in Berea as nobler than those of Thessalonica. This is due not just to the readiness with which they accepted the gospel, but also the diligence with which they searched the scriptures in order to confirm the authenticity of what they had been taught.

It is my prayer that this book will be a source of blessing to all who have come to the knowledge of Christ and have a hunger and desire to worship God and live a successful Christian life.

NOW THAT YOU HAVE RECEIVED CHRIST

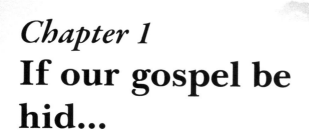

Chapter 1
If our gospel be hid...

Receiving Christ is the most amazing and liberating experience anyone can have. However, it takes many of us so many years and lots of agonising moments before we arrive at the decision to accept Him.

Growing up as a child, I remember myself being a very thoughtful person. Like most other children at the time, I also played pranks and engaged in many acts of truancy, but deep down within me I always wanted to do the right thing, please my parents and, ultimately, please God.

My siblings and I were brought up in church and had

to attend children's Sunday school. Our prayer time at home involved extensive Bible reading and we always read a chapter of the Psalms in Yoruba. We memorised so many chapters of Psalms. The prayers were sometimes so long that we would have fallen asleep by the time it ended. Throughout this time, I had not consciously given my life to Christ, and although we all were seen as Christians, I didn't have a relationship with Jesus.

At an early stage I started to question a lot of things happening in the church, particularly with the older generation, even though I couldn't possibly express my opinion. I found it strange when adults tell children not to lie but then ask the same children to cover up for them. A popular one was asking children to tell visitors that they were asleep or not at home.

My older sister was the first in our family to receive Christ as her Lord and Saviour. She had always been the gentlest and kindest of us all. I actually cannot remember her engaging in any of our silly vices. After she gave her life to Christ, I knew there was something different about her, even though at the time I didn't realise it was the presence of the Holy Spirit. She did her best to tell us about Christ but I couldn't comprehend the whole idea.

On one occasion I even said the sinner's prayer, but there was no change in my life. It is essential for us to realise that God has done everything that needs to be done for the salvation of mankind. He gave His only Son as an atoning sacrifice for our sins and this sacrifice is a once-and-for-all sacrifice. Jesus stated this clearly when He said:

For God so loved the world, that he gave his only begotten Son, that whosoever believeth in him should not perish, but have everlasting life. (John 3:16)

Receiving Christ as Lord and Saviour is a spiritual exercise, and we struggle to understand the gospel and its message because the enemy of our soul blinds people's minds. Until this blindness is removed we cannot understand the Gospel message. The Apostle Paul gives us some insight into this:

But if our gospel be hid, it is hid to them that are lost: in whom the god of this world hath blinded the minds of them which believe not, lest the light of the glorious gospel of Christ, who is the image of God, should shine unto them. (2 Corinthians 4:3-4)

The sacrifice of Christ on the cross at Calvary is an all-encompassing sacrifice for the sin of the whole world.

He has done everything that needs to be done in order to satisfy God's judgement, and for the deliverance of every human being who will pass through the face of the earth. Each one of us only needs to accept Christ's sacrifice and appropriate this in our lives. In the same vein, when praying for any loved one who has not accepted Christ Jesus as their Lord and Saviour, our prayer shouldn't be for God to save them, for this He has already done, but that the veil that has so far covered their eyes be removed so that they might see the light of the glorious gospel of our Lord and so accept Him as Lord and Saviour.

It took at least another six or seven years after I first heard the gospel through my sister before I fully understood its message and committed my life to Christ. A lot happened during this period, but I am glad to say that He found me in a most amazing way and I gave my life to Him. Family members prayed for my salvation and I am glad their prayers were answered.

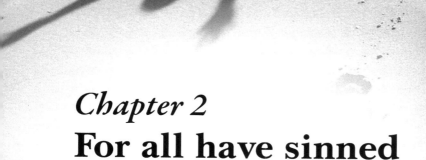

Chapter 2
For all have sinned

*For all have sinned, and come short of the glory of God...
(Romans 3:23)*

*Being able to recognise that we are sinners who have
fallen short of God's glory is the starting point of our
journey to salvation and ultimately to God's kingdom.
As simple as this might sound, a lot of people struggle
to understand it. We cannot obtain God's forgiveness
until we acknowledge our sin, repent of it and ask for
forgiveness. The Bible presents a dialogue between Jesus
and His critics as follows:*

And when the Pharisees saw it, they said unto his

disciples, Why eateth your Master with publicans and sinners? But when Jesus heard that, he said unto them, They that be whole need not a physician, but they that are sick. But go ye and learn what that meaneth, I will have mercy, and not sacrifice: for I am not come to call the righteous, but sinners to repentance. (Matthew 9: 11–13)

In the passage above, the Pharisees despised Jesus because of His relationship with sinners, but Jesus made it clear that He did not come to rescue the self-righteous. His ministry is, however, to those who are humble enough to acknowledge their sin.

Sin here does not necessarily refer to the occasional transgression of the law but the nature of sin that every human being inherited from our ancestors, Adam and Eve, when they sinned in the Garden of Eden. We are therefore sinners not because we lie, cheat, steal or do other things that are against God's law, but because we have the nature of sin which gives us the inherent ability to do wrong. David recognised this and he made the following comment in one of his psalms:

Behold, I was shapen in iniquity; and in sin did my mother conceive me. (Psalm 51:5)

Paul the Apostle also gave an insight into this in the Book of Romans:

For as by one man's disobedience many were made sinners, so by the obedience of one shall many be made righteous. (Romans 5:19)

We are not sinners because we sin but we sin because we are sinners. The unregenerate man is like a sin factory and cannot help but sin until he receives deliverance from Christ. But as sure as we inherited sin from Adam without having personally or individually done anything, we will also most certainly obtain righteousness from the Lord Jesus Christ as soon as we embrace Him and accept His sacrifice for us on the cross of Calvary.

The second and equally important part of our opening scripture is that we have all fallen short of the glory of God. If like me you have an enquiring mind, you may wish to understand what the glory of God is and why it is so grave to have fallen short of it.

If we cast our mind back to the story of the parents of the human race (Adam and Eve) as recorded in the Book of Genesis, we will recollect that they were in the Garden and were naked but not ashamed (Genesis

2:25). However, this sense of innocence and security that they had was damaged due to disobedience, such that they became vulnerable and insecure (Genesis 3:7-10). The glory of God is therefore His divine covering on man that shields man from the evils of the world and makes us pure and secure. The glory is restored to us when we receive Christ as our Lord and Saviour. Paul wrote:

Therefore if any man be in Christ, he is a new creature: old things are passed away; behold, all things are become new. (2 Corinthians 5:17)

Despite the fact that I grew up going to church and attending Sunday school, for the first 20 years of my life I never fully understood how, as a sinner, I had fallen short of the glory of God. As a result, I didn't see the need for me to embrace God's love and sacrifice for my sin. I, like many other people who lived around me, compared myself with others and always felt I wasn't doing too badly. However, it got to a point in my life when I never really cared, as I was occupied with my own selfish interests. This is a dangerous place to be, but I bless God for all those who prayed for me, asking Him to open my eyes to see the light of His glorious gospel.

For every reader who has not received Christ as Lord and Saviour, I pray that God in His love and kindness will open your eyes to recognise your state of sinfulness, so that you can have that sense of deep need of God's mercy and forgiveness that is required for salvation.

Chapter 3
Eternal life

For the wages of sin is death; but the gift of God is eternal life through Jesus Christ our Lord. (Romans 6:23)

In the previous chapter, emphasis was laid on the need to recognise and acknowledge the presence of sin in man. This recognition is, however, only the beginning of the journey towards salvation. The presence and perpetuation of sin has a grave consequence for us all – death.

Death here does not refer to the physical death which occurs when a human being's life on earth terminates, but to a separation from God's presence and fellowship which can be referred to as spiritual death.

In the story of Adam and Eve, as recorded in the Book of Genesis, God had warned Adam that he mustn't eat of the tree of knowledge of good and evil. If he did, he would die. Adam and Eve didn't die physically after their disobedience of eating from the forbidden tree, they died spiritually: they became separated from God. The fellowship they had with God prior to their sin was broken. All human beings are destined to experience this kind of death unless they accept Jesus Christ as their Saviour, for He is the one who God has given as the perfect and sufficient atoning sacrifice for the world's sin. Paul explains:

For since by man came death, by man came also the resurrection of the dead. For as in Adam all die, even so in Christ shall all be made alive.
(1 Corinthians 15:21-22)

When Satan deceived the human race, he must have thought that he had thwarted God's purpose for man. At this time, Satan had already rebelled against God and as a result received God's eternal judgement. Following his rebellion and subsequent fall from God's favour, he plotted to defile the wonderful creation that God had made in His own image.

Unfortunately, man fell into Satan's trap, but thankfully God already had a redemptive plan for man. The first man (Adam) sinned and died spiritually as a result of his sin, and all who have descended from Adam have inherited his sinful nature and the sentence of death that goes with it. Amazingly, as a result of the obedience of Christ, we now have the option of salvation and eternal life. This is confirmed in Romans:

> *For as by one man's disobedience many were made sinners, so by the obedience of one shall many be made righteous.* (Romans 5:19)

Our opening text in this chapter declares that God's gift is eternal life through Jesus Christ our Lord. It is clear from this scripture that this gift is not automatic. It can only come into effect in the lives of those who accept the glorious gospel by yielding themselves to God by accepting Jesus. Taking this wonderful step elevates us to the position of sonship through adoption into God's own family. This is confirmed by the following passages:

> *He was in the world, and the world was made by him, and the world knew him not. He came*

unto his own, and his own received him not. But as many as received him, to them gave he power to become the sons of God, even to them that believe on his name... (John 1:10-12)

Who hath delivered us from the power of darkness, and hath translated us into the kingdom of his dear Son... (Colossians 1:13)

Anyone who has taken this amazing step has every reason to rejoice and be grateful to the Almighty God who has purchased eternal life for us. Eternal life is not something we are going to receive in the future, but something we already have now because we believe in the name of Jesus and have accepted Him as our Lord and Saviour. And it does not matter whether we had a dramatic salvation experience like Saul of Tarsus or a quiet serene encounter. As long as we genuinely received Him, we have eternal life. This is confirmed in the following passages:

These things have I written unto you that believe on the name of the Son of God; that ye may know that ye have eternal life, and that ye may believe on the name of the Son of God. (1 John 5:13)

These words spake Jesus, and lifted up his eyes to heaven, and said, Father, the hour is come; glorify thy Son, that thy Son also may glorify thee: as thou hast given him power over all flesh, that he should give eternal life to as many as thou hast given him. And this is life eternal, that they might know thee the only true God, and Jesus Christ, whom thou hast sent. (John 17:1-3)

If you are reading this book and you have not already experienced this eternal life, I pray that God's love will overwhelm you and you will recognise Him as the only true God, and accept His Son Jesus as your Lord and Saviour.

In the following chapter, I will recount my salvation experience and it is my prayer that my testimony will be a blessing and source of deliverance to someone reading it.

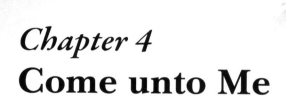

Chapter 4
Come unto Me

Come unto me, all ye that labour and are heavy laden, and I will give you rest. (Matthew 11:28)

It was in my final year in the university when the Lord found me. I had lost my father when I was fifteen in a most traumatic way.

We'd left home together that fateful morning and we were being chauffeur-driven to the bank, where my dad stopped to see the manager. I went off with the driver to buy some things with the hope of returning to pick up my dad. Unfortunately, by the time we got to the bank, the manager had asked his own driver to take my dad home. My dad saw us arriving at the bank just as he was leaving and he beckoned to us to follow him in our car, which we did.

We arrived home just after him and I saw him get out of the manager's car. Our driver drove to the back of the house, where he intended to drop off the things we had purchased, while I got out to meet my dad at the front of our house. Suddenly, I saw a man rush out of a white vehicle that had driven very fast into our street. He was carrying a gun and he took aim at my dad, and in what appeared to be seconds, my dad was shot and the man ran back into the waiting car and disappeared.

The driver and I immediately struggled to get my dad into the car and we drove really fast to the hospital, and I can still remember his last words in my native Yoruba language: "O ti tan", meaning, "It is finished." While driving to the hospital, I cried desperately to God to preserve my dad's life, so you can guess how devastated and heartbroken I was when the doctor pronounced him dead at the hospital. My life was completely torn apart and I became distraught, trying desperately to wish the experience away. I would describe my dad as a very good man, not just because he was my dad but because he had a very good heart – which many have attested to in the years since he died.

The next few years of my life were difficult and bitter

even though, externally, I did my best to pretend that everything was alright. I had so much love and respect for my mum, who worked tirelessly to ensure that we were all properly brought up, even when it meant that she had to deprive herself of a lot of comforts in life.

Following the tragedy of my dad passing away, I started getting involved in drinking, smoking and other ugly acts, but because of the respect I had for my mum, I did my best to keep all these things secret from her. But eventually, I got tired of smoking cigarettes and started craving other substances, and as it happened one morning during my final year in university, I visited some friends and joined them in smoking marijuana. After we had finished smoking, everything was okay – until I decided to go home. As soon as I left the friend's house and set out for mine, I started hearing voices. A voice asked me to take off my clothes and another asked me to start marching. It felt strange and I started questioning the voices. It turned out to be the beginning of an ugly spiritual experience that lasted for what must have been a month or two.

In desperation, I visited some independent African spiritualist churches. By now it was no longer just about the voices, but also some strange feelings and sensations all over my body. I eventually went home and told my mum about my problems, leading us to visit more spiritualist churches in search of a solution. I am not sure when it was during the whole episode that I heard another voice, asking me to read the Bible. I argued with this voice, stating that "the Bible is such a huge book" and that I was sure that something bad would happen to me before I found answers for my situation in the Bible. Thankfully, the same voice said to me, "Start from the New Testament" – and that was how I began reading the Bible.

I can still remember getting to Matthew 11:28-29 where the Lord said, "Come unto me, all ye that labour and are heavy laden, and I will give you rest." I knelt beside my bed and cried to God, asking Him to deliver me from my troubles. I remember promising Him that I would never return to my old ways if He delivered me. I still remember the brightness in my room and the singing that I heard in my spirit.

I wasn't sure what had happened to me, but I remembered sharing my experience with my cousin, who was my flatmate at the time, and asking him to accompany me to the Christian Union Fellowship on campus. Prior to my experience, I had been invited on several occasions to the Fellowship and had refused to attend. But as the Lord would have it, I attended the Fellowship, where I was prayed for and admonished, and told not to return to any of the spiritualist churches. I also formally gave my life to Christ and that marked the end of the unusual experiences, as well as the eerie sensations that I'd felt in my body.

I continued reading the Bible and soon completed the New Testament. Then I started from the beginning, in the Book of Genesis, and read right through to Revelation. It was the best period of my life, as the Lord took me through the most amazing journey, reading through the Bible. There were moments of pure joy when the Lord dropped revelations from His Word into my heart.

Chapter 5
Work out your salvation

Wherefore, my beloved, as ye have always obeyed, not as in my presence only, but now much more in my absence, work out your own salvation with fear and trembling. For it is God which worketh in you both to will and to do of his good pleasure. Do all things without murmurings and disputings: that ye may be blameless and harmless, the sons of God, without rebuke, in the midst of a crooked and perverse nation, among whom ye shine as lights in the world...
(Philippians 2:12-15)

I often say to people whenever I have the opportunity to teach along this line that there is 'salvation' after salvation.

As funny as it may sound, the journey of salvation does not end with decision to be saved. There is a working out that each child of God must do after they have received Jesus as Lord and Saviour. The salvation that we obtain at the point of receiving Jesus is what I will refer to here as the entry point of salvation. We cannot however remain here, we have to make progress, and this progression is what must be worked out with fear and trembling. This must be done in total surrender to God, as it is only through the help of His Holy Spirit that we can live a blameless and harmless life in the midst of such a crooked and perverse generation.

After hearing the message of the gospel through direct evangelism, reading of the Word, observing the lifestyle of another Christian or through the mass media, we decide whether or not to agree with the message. Those who agree with and embrace the message obtain God's gift of salvation. If such a person dies afterwards, he or she will go to heaven. Such a person may not have displayed excellence in their character up till the moment of their death, but because they have accepted Christ, their sins have been forgiven and they are declared guiltless by God.

We know, however, that in reality few of us die straight after we have become Christians. It might seem logical, in our eyes, that the best possible time for God to take people to heaven would be immediately after they are saved and their sins have been washed away. But God doesn't seem to work that way for most of us – we continue to live in this world with all its temptations. Jesus, recognising that this could pose a challenge, prayed for all who would be in this position:

> *I pray not that thou shouldest take them out of the world, but that thou shouldest keep them from the evil.* (John 17:15)

He did not pray that the Father would take those who believe out of the world, but that He would keep us from evil. This is because He has an assignment for us here on earth. He wants us to be His representatives, particularly in the area of soul winning (the ministry of reconciliation). Paul emphasised this to the Corinthians:

> *And all things are of God, who hath reconciled us to himself by Jesus Christ, and hath given to us the ministry of reconciliation; to wit, that God was in Christ, reconciling the world unto himself, not*

imputing their trespasses unto them; and hath committed unto us the word of reconciliation. Now then we are ambassadors for Christ, as though God did beseech you by us: we pray you in Christ's stead, be ye reconciled to God. (2 Corinthians 5:18-20)

A lot of believers do not have any clarity concerning the next steps they should take after receiving Jesus as their Lord and Saviour. They do not have a clear direction about what is expected of them, and so a lot of people experience various levels of avoidable struggles.

I still remember seeking guidance and direction from mature Christians around me. It can be disheartening when a sermon describes to people what is expected of them without explaining how such expectations can be achieved. As a young Christian, I often met with ministers privately, asking them to teach me how the things they had described could be achieved.

It is therefore my hope that we will be able to learn in the following chapters, through the guidance of the Holy Spirit, what we need to do in order to work out our salvation. This is very important, because the way we live our lives and conduct our activities following our salvation determines how effective we are in our Christianity, and can also affect the impression we have on other people around us. More importantly, it will determine whether at the end of our race we will receive a commendation or condemnation. Our Lord alluded to this in the parable of the talents:

And so he that had received five talents came and brought other five talents, saying, Lord, thou deliveredst unto me five talents: behold, I have gained beside them five talents more. His lord said unto him, Well done, thou good and faithful servant: thou hast been faithful over a few things, I will make thee ruler over many things: enter thou into the joy of thy lord... Then he which had received the one talent came and said, Lord, I knew thee that thou art an hard man, reaping where thou hast not sown, and gathering where thou hast not strawed: and I was afraid, and went and hid thy talent in the earth: lo, there thou hast that is thine. His lord answered and said unto him, Thou wicked and slothful servant, thou knewest that I reap where I sowed not, and gather where I have not strawed: thou oughtest therefore to have put my money to the exchangers, and then at my coming

I should have received mine own with usury. Take therefore the talent from him, and give it unto him which hath ten talents. For unto every one that hath shall be given, and he shall have abundance: but from him that hath not shall be taken away even that which he hath. And cast ye the unprofitable servant into outer darkness: there shall be weeping and gnashing of teeth. (Matthew 25:24-30)

Chapter 6
As ye have therefore received Christ Jesus

As ye have therefore received Christ Jesus the Lord, so walk ye in him: rooted and built up in him, and stablished in the faith, as ye have been taught, abounding therein with thanksgiving. (Colossians 2:6-7)

It is very clear from these verses that the first step that must be taken in our journey of faith is accepting Christ Jesus as Lord. This is crucial because, as Lord, He must have total control over our lives. He must be consulted over every decision and He must rule in every situation.

This can only be achieved if, after receiving Jesus into our lives, we live a life of total surrender to Him. To help us in this, Paul lists the steps that we must take when starting out on our new life with Christ. His instruction can be broken down into the following points:

1. Walk in Him (Jesus)
2. Be rooted and built up in Him
3. Be established in Him
4. Abound in Him with thanksgiving

1. WALKING IN JESUS

This implies that we must continue to seek guidance from Him and follow Him, and how else can we seek His guidance if not through His Word?

It is interesting how a lot of us want to hear God speak to us audibly, but we refuse to dip ourselves into His Word through diligent study. If we desire to hear God speak to us audibly, we must first of all hear Him through His Word. Our spiritual senses will then be sharpened enough to hear Him audibly.

When we receive Christ Jesus as Lord, our spirit becomes born again and, just like any new-born babe, our spirit requires nourishment in order to grow. The human spirit is, however, not nourished by our usual diet but by the Word of God. Whereas food nourishes the body, the Word of God nourishes the spirit. Apostle Peter explained this as follows:

> *As newborn babes, desire the sincere milk of the word, that ye may grow thereby...* (1 Peter 2:2)

He wrote to encourage young Christians to desire or long for the pure milk of God's Word so that they may grow. I am sure you know that before a baby can walk, it would have received enough nourishment through the parents and grown to the age when it is able to walk. In the same way, a Christian should absorb the Word of God through all the available means, which may include attending church and listening to sermons, going to Sunday school or Bible study classes, completing discipleship courses, or personally studying the Word.

In his charge to Joshua, God emphasised the need for personal study of His Word and even pointed out that Joshua's success depended on it:

> *This book of the law shall not depart out of thy mouth;*

but thou shalt meditate therein day and night, that thou mayest observe to do according to all that is written therein: for then thou shalt make thy way prosperous, and then thou shalt have good success. (Joshua 1:8)

The instruction to Joshua included continuous study and confession of the Word, daily meditation and obedience to its instructions. Doing this will guarantee success, not just for Joshua but for every believer who follows this divine instruction. David wrote in agreement with this in the first Psalm, and also detailed how anyone who desires God's blessedness must not walk:

Blessed is the man that walketh not in the counsel of the ungodly, nor standeth in the way of sinners, nor sitteth in the seat of the scornful. But his delight is in the law of the LORD; and in his law doth he meditate day and night. And he shall be like a tree planted by the rivers of water, that bringeth forth his fruit in his season; his leaf also shall not wither; and whatsoever he doeth shall prosper. (Psalm 1:1-3)

Prosperity doesn't come through laziness but through diligence in the study of God's Word and obedience to it.

Once this is attained, there is a need to have fellowship with God through prayer. It is clear from the Word of God that He desires us to walk with Him in fellowship. In fact, God literally walked with man in the Garden of Eden before Adam and Eve sinned. The Bible records:

> *And they heard the voice of the LORD God walking in the garden in the cool of the day: and Adam and his wife hid themselves from the presence of the LORD God amongst the trees of the garden.* (Genesis 3:8)

God was walking in the Garden, seeking man's fellowship, but the first couple sinned and lost this wonderful fellowship with God.

One man in the scriptures, however, found the secret of walking with God. The name of this man is Enoch. You can literally picture him having a stroll with God and having deep conversations with Him. Enoch did this for 300 years, and God must have enjoyed the fellowship so much that he took Enoch home with Him by making Enoch bypass death. The Bible says:

> *And Enoch walked with God after he begat Methuselah three hundred years, and begat sons and*

daughters: and all the days of Enoch were three
hundred sixty and five years: and Enoch walked
with God: and he was not; for God took him.
(Genesis 5:22-24)

Abraham also had a close walk with God, such
that he was declared a friend of God. In fact, when
God was going to destroy the cities of Sodom and
Gomorrah, He decided that He must consult with
Abraham before He proceeded on His mission.
This is recorded in Genesis 18:17-18:

And the LORD said, Shall I hide from Abraham that
thing which I do; seeing that Abraham shall surely
become a great and mighty nation, and all the nations
of the earth shall be blessed in him?

Another important point to note here is that God
is Spirit and, for this reason, He communicates
with us through our spirit. Our spirit becomes
born again when we receive Christ. God also gives
us His Holy Spirit as a guarantee and assurance
of our salvation and He resides in us. If we then
nourish our spirit by feeding it with the Word of
God, our conscience – which is the voice of our

spirit – becomes very sensitive to God's Holy Spirit. With this line of communication between our spirit and God open, it becomes easier for us to hear Him whenever He speaks to us.

Paul the Apostle gives us an insight into this in the following verses:

> *For what man knoweth the things of a man, save the spirit of man which is in him? Even so the things of God knoweth no man, but the Spirit of God. Now we have received, not the spirit of the world, but the spirit which is of God; that we might know the things that are freely given to us of God. Which things also we speak, not in the words which man's wisdom teacheth, but which the Holy Ghost teacheth; comparing spiritual things with spiritual. But the natural man receiveth not the things of the Spirit of God: for they are foolishness unto him: neither can he know them, because they are spiritually discerned. But he that is spiritual judgeth all things, yet he himself is judged of no man. For who hath known the mind of the Lord, that he may instruct him? But we have the mind of Christ.* (1 Corinthians 2:11–16)

It is mind-blowing to comprehend the things described

by Paul in the above scripture. Isn't it amazing that if we diligently pursue the things of God and become "spiritually discerning" we will have the mind of Christ? We will think like He thinks and do what He does.

It is my prayer that every reader of this book will develop a close relationship with God through a daily study of the Word and prayer.

2. BEING ROOTED AND BUILT UP IN JESUS

Being rooted and becoming built up in Jesus will be considered together here because of their interrelationship.

Taking root in Jesus involves making sure He is the foundation of everything we do and connecting firmly to Him. This is very important because every Christian requires a solid foundation to build upon and, as clearly declared by Paul the Apostle, Jesus is that foundation that we all must build on. Hear him:

> *According to the grace of God which is given unto me, as a wise masterbuilder, I have laid the foundation, and another buildeth thereon. But let every man take heed how he buildeth thereupon. For other foundation can no man lay than that is laid, which is Jesus Christ.* (1 Corinthians 3:10-11)

Every wise builder digs deep and prepares a solid base or firm foundation for whatever structure they plan to build. This is done in order to ensure that the building will stand firm and survive any storm that is thrown at it. In the previous heading, our walk with God was narrowed down to two main Christian disciplines: studying the Word and prayer. The result of diligently following both disciplines for any Christian will be hearing God. If you study the Word of God after receiving Him as Lord and Saviour, His Word will minister to your spirit and you will hear Him speak to you. In the same way, when you fellowship with God in prayer, He will speak to you and give you clear directions.

There is, however, a clear distinction between hearing God and doing His will. Anyone who seeks to be rooted and built up in Him will not only hear Him but also obey Him. Jesus expounded on this in one of His parables to His disciples:

> *Therefore whosoever heareth these sayings of mine, and doeth them, I will liken him unto a wise man, which built his house upon a rock: and the rain descended, and the floods came, and the winds blew, and beat upon that house; and it fell not: for it was founded upon a rock. And every one that heareth these sayings of mine, and doeth them not, shall be likened unto a*

foolish man, which built his house upon the sand: and
the rain descended, and the floods came, and the winds
blew, and beat upon that house; and it fell: and great
was the fall of it. (Matthew 7:24-27)

From the passage above, our faith in God, which must
be clearly demonstrated by our obedience to Him, must
be so solidly grounded that the storms of life will not be
able to move us. This solid faith is built up by a knowledge
of God through His Word for "faith cometh by hearing,
and hearing by the word of God" (Romans 10:17). We
have a personal responsibility of paying attention to
His Word and guarding our heart so that we do not
become corrupted by error that is presented as the truth.
Traditions of men and philosophical teaching which
appeal to our common sense, but are clearly not the
Word of God, will destroy our faith. We must avoid
them, warned Apostle Paul:

Beware lest any man spoil you through philosophy
and vain deceit, after the tradition of men, after
the rudiments of the world, and not after Christ.
(Colossians 2:8)

I cannot overemphasise the need for believers to hear

God for themselves and be led by the Holy Spirit, as this is vital to the success of any believer's walk with God. It is true that God has given us pastors, prophets, evangelists and teachers so that they can equip us, but it is equally true and highly important that He has given us His Spirit. Romans 8:14 tells us that "... as many as are led by the Spirit of God, they are the sons of God."

I have often asked myself why God decided to give His Spirit to every believer, and one of the main reasons that I have found is this: so that He can have a personal relationship with each individual Christian. If we trust and rely on the Holy Spirit enough, we will not be easily deceived by anyone because He is the Spirit of truth, who the Father has given to us so that He can reveal His truth to us:

> *And I will pray the Father, and he shall give you another Comforter, that he may abide with you for ever; even the Spirit of truth; whom the world cannot receive, because it seeth him not, neither knoweth him: but ye know him; for he dwelleth with you, and shall be in you. I will not leave you comfortless: I will come to you. Yet a little while, and the world seeth me no more; but ye see me: because I live, ye shall live also. At that day ye shall know that I am in my*

*Father, and ye in me, and I in you. He that hath my
commandments, and keepeth them, he it is that loveth
me: and he that loveth me shall be loved of my Father,
and I will love him, and will manifest myself to him.*
(John 14:16-21)

It is interesting that Jesus did not just promise to give us
the Spirit of truth who will make known His mind to
us. He went on to emphasise the need for us to obey His
commands, as this is the only way we can demonstrate
our love for Him. If we can do this successfully, He
promises to love us in return and then manifest or reveal
Himself to us. However, this is not the end of the story,
for Jesus continued to explain, in John chapters 15 and
16, other important things that the Spirit of truth will
accomplish in the life of a believer:

*But when the Comforter is come, whom I will send
unto you from the Father, even the Spirit of truth,
which proceedeth from the Father, he shall testify of
me...*(John 15:26)

*Howbeit when he, the Spirit of truth, is come, he
will guide you into all truth: for he shall not speak
of himself; but whatsoever he shall hear, that shall he
speak: and he will shew you things to come. He shall*

glorify me: for he shall receive of mine, and shall shew it unto you. All things that the Father hath are mine: therefore said I, that he shall take of mine, and shall shew it unto you. (John 16:13-15)

I had a personal experience with the Spirit of truth following my encounter with the Lord (receiving Christ as my Lord and Saviour). Whenever I listened to a sermon or a message, I would hear a confirmation in my spirit if what was being said was correct. I would also hear in my spirit a loud and clear NO whenever what was being said was incorrect. It was interesting how Scriptures were brought to my remembrance in support of the correctness or otherwise of any aspect of the message.

I enjoyed going through my Bible to confirm these things whenever I was on my own. Some people think everything that is said from the pulpit must be correct and even consider it sinful to think otherwise. I do not agree with this line of thinking. While I don't subscribe to any believer challenging a preacher or teacher concerning their message, we are not compelled to accept the content of any message. In fact, the people of Berea were commended because they did not accept every message hook, line and sinker. Luke recorded this for us in the Acts of the Apostles:

And the brethren immediately sent away Paul and Silas by night unto Berea: who coming thither went into the synagogue of the Jews. These were more noble than those in Thessalonica, in that they received the word with all readiness of mind, and searched the scriptures daily, whether those things were so. (Acts 17:10-11)

While these groups of people received the word with all readiness of mind, they also diligently searched the scriptures to confirm whether or not what they had been taught was true. It is our personal responsibility to ensure that the spiritual nutrition we are fed with is unadulterated. Apostle Peter described it in 1 Peter 2:2 as "the sincere milk of the word".

It is clear from all the scriptures we have considered that being rooted and built up in Christ entails knowing the will of God, and basing every decision in our life on His instructions and directions. Everything we do in life must be as led by the Spirit of God, since this is the only sure way to demonstrate that we are God's children (Romans 8:14). Just like Paul the Apostle, I would like to commend you to a life of pursuit and obedience of God's Word. In line with the words of Paul the Apostle, I would also like to commend you to a life of prayer, as these are the keys to becoming rooted and built up in Christ. Paul encouraged the disciples with the following words:

> *And now, brethren, I commend you to God, and to the word of his grace, which is able to build you up, and to give you an inheritance among all them which are sanctified.* (Acts 20:32)

Jude informed his listeners to build themselves up:

> *But ye, beloved, building up yourselves on your most holy faith, praying in the Holy Ghost...* (Jude 1:20)

3. BECOMING ESTABLISHED IN JESUS

We have spent a bit of time highlighting the need to maintain a close fellowship with God through the study of His Word, obedience to His instruction and prayer. Like any other venture in life, there must be a way of measuring success. In this instance, growth becomes an essential means of measuring progress and success in our relationship with Christ. A quick look at the scripture that opened this chapter will be helpful to our understanding of becoming established or growing in Christ. It stated:

Rooted and built up in him, and stablished in the faith, as ye have been taught, abounding therein with thanksgiving. (Colossians 2:7)

The word used here is 'stablished' which means to stabilise or make stable. It is key to note that it says a new believer should strive to become stabilised in the faith. When we commence any new venture, we take time to learn its basics, until we become experts in the venture. I am sure that any normal mother or father expects their children to grow, and it would be a matter of concern if a child did not make any effort to crawl, walk or talk by the time it was two years old or above. At various stages in a human life there are clear expectations of physical and mental developments. In the same way, after having been taught by pastors and teachers, whilst at the same time studying the Word of God and praying, there is an expectation that a believer will grow to become established or more knowledgeable in the faith.

The writer of Hebrews wrote about an expectation

that believers will grow up to full age and become teachers themselves:

> *For when for the time ye ought to be teachers, ye have need that one teach you again which be the first principles of the oracles of God; and are become such as have need of milk, and not of strong meat. For every one that useth milk is unskilful in the word of righteousness: for he is a babe. But strong meat belongeth to them that are of full age, even those who by reason of use have their senses exercised to discern both good and evil.* (Hebrews 5:12-14)

In what areas should we therefore expect growth in the life of a believer? There are two clear areas of growth defined by Peter the Apostle in his epistle, which are grace and the knowledge of Jesus:

> *But grow in grace, and in the knowledge of our Lord and Saviour Jesus Christ. To him be glory both now and for ever. Amen.* (2 Peter 3:18)

Some areas of grace that we are expected to grow

in are listed below. (Please note that this list is not exhaustive.)

1. Growth in the knowledge and understanding of the Word

Let the word of Christ dwell in you richly in all wisdom; teaching and admonishing one another in psalms and hymns and spiritual songs, singing with grace in your hearts to the Lord. (Colossians 3:16)

Growing in the knowledge and understanding of God's Word requires prayerful study and meditation on the Word through the help of the Holy Spirit. We also learn and retain a lot when we fellowship with other brothers and sisters, teaching and learning from each other.

2. Growth in faith

This is essential for our walk with God, as without faith we cannot please God. Jesus' disciples recognised the need to grow in this area so they prayed for an increase in faith. The Bible says:

*But without faith it is impossible to please him: for he
that cometh to God must believe that he is, and that
he is a rewarder of them that diligently seek him.*
(Hebrews 11:6)

And the apostles said unto the Lord, Increase our faith.
(Luke 17:5)

3. Growth in teaching and evangelism

One major reason that God does not take believers
away from the world after saving them is that He
wants them to be His ambassadors, reaching out to
the unsaved people of the world, teaching them and
reconciling them to Him. In fact, after He rose, Jesus
gave his followers a charge that is now known as the
Great Commission. This is clearly depicted by Matthew
in his account:

*Go ye therefore, and teach all nations, baptizing them
in the name of the Father, and of the Son, and of
the Holy Ghost: teaching them to observe all things
whatsoever I have commanded you: and, lo, I am
with you always, even unto the end of the world.
Amen.* (Matthew 28:19–20)

This charge to teach and evangelise isn't just for leaders or ministers of the gospel but for every believer. I particularly like the way Paul the Apostle describes the ministry that we received following our belief in Christ – the ministry of reconciliation and the duty of ambassadors. He said:

> *Therefore if any man be in Christ, he is a new creature: old things are passed away; behold, all things are become new. And all things are of God, who hath reconciled us to himself by Jesus Christ, and hath given to us the ministry of reconciliation; to wit, that God was in Christ, reconciling the world unto himself, not imputing their trespasses unto them; and hath committed unto us the word of reconciliation. Now then we are ambassadors for Christ, as though God did beseech you by us: we pray you in Christ's stead, be ye reconciled to God.* (2 Corinthians 5:17-20)

In Jesus' own words we glorify God through our evangelistic fruitfulness. He stated:

> *Herein is my Father glorified, that ye bear much fruit; so shall ye be my disciples.* (John 15:8)

4. Growth in prayer

In order to ensure success in ministry, the early apostles appointed deacons to deal with some administrative issues so that they could devote themselves to prayer:

> *But we will give ourselves continually to prayer, and to the ministry of the word.* (Acts 6:4)

They must have learnt the importance of this kind of lifestyle from Jesus, who devoted much of His ministry to prayer and encouraged His followers to do the same. A few scriptures on prayer are highlighted below:

> *And in the morning, rising up a great while before day, he went out, and departed into a solitary place, and there prayed.* (Mark 1:35)

> *And he spake a parable unto them to this end, that men ought always to pray, and not to faint...* (Luke 18:1)

> *Praying always with all prayer and supplication in the Spirit, and watching thereunto with all perseverance and supplication for all saints...* (Ephesians 6:18)

5. Growth in the grace of giving

One of the ways we demonstrate our commitment to God is through the giving of our substance not just to God but also to our fellow men. Consider the example in the following passage:

Moreover, brethren, we do you to wit of the grace of God bestowed on the churches of Macedonia; how that in a great trial of affliction the abundance of their joy and their deep poverty abounded unto the riches of their liberality. For to their power, I bear record, yea, and beyond their power they were willing of themselves; praying us with much intreaty that we would receive the gift, and take upon us the fellowship of the ministering to the saints. And this they did, not as we hoped, but first gave their own selves to the Lord, and unto us by the will of God. Insomuch that we desired Titus, that as he had begun, so he would also finish in you the same grace also. Therefore, as ye abound in every thing, in faith, and utterance, and knowledge, and in all diligence, and in your love to us, see that ye abound in this grace also. I speak not by commandment, but by occasion of the forwardness of others, and to prove the sincerity of your love. For ye know the grace of our Lord Jesus Christ, that, though he was rich, yet for your sakes

*he became poor, that ye through his poverty might
be rich.* (2 Corinthians 8:1-9)

The grace of giving appears to be the most taught about
in Christian circles today and has as such been open to
abuse. If, however, we take time to prayerfully understand
it, this grace can also be an amazing blessing to the
Body of Christ. Paul the Apostle encouraged believers
in Corinth to abound in this grace, just as they had in
other areas of their faith.

6. Growth in love

Understanding love and walking in it is critical to
the Christian faith. In His summation of God's
commandments, Jesus told His disciples that love
is central. He also emphasised that the test of true
discipleship is love:

*Master, which is the great commandment in the
law? Jesus said unto him, Thou shalt love the Lord
thy God with all thy heart, and with all thy soul,
and with all thy mind. This is the first and great
commandment. And the second is like unto it, Thou
shalt love thy neighbour as thyself. On these two*

*commandments hang all the law and the prophets.
(Matthew 22:36–40)*

*By this shall all men know that ye are my disciples, if
ye have love one to another.* (John 13:35)

4. ABOUNDING IN THANKSGIVING

The final subject we will be looking at in this section is
thanksgiving. This also happens to be an area of grace
because we need the help of the Holy Spirit in order
to succeed in it.

In his letter to the Thessalonians, we are admonished by
Paul the Apostle to give thanks in everything because
this is God's will for us (1 Thessalonians 5:18). This is
one area that can be easily dismissed and considered
ridiculous, for how can we be expected to give thanks
when faced with terrible situations? We will only be able
to fully comprehend this grace when we look closely at
the lives of believers that have gone ahead of us. Paul
himself passed through various difficult and extremely
challenging situations but he continued to give thanks
to God. He confirmed:

We are troubled on every side, yet not distressed; we

are perplexed, but not in despair; persecuted, but not forsaken; cast down, but not destroyed; always bearing about in the body the dying of the Lord Jesus, that the life also of Jesus might be made manifest in our body. For we which live are always delivered unto death for Jesus' sake, that the life also of Jesus might be made manifest in our mortal flesh. So then death worketh in us, but life in you... For all things are for your sakes, that the abundant grace might through the thanksgiving of many redound to the glory of God. (2 Corinthians 4:8-12,15)

Paul was clearly not asking us to do what he has not done himself. The resultant effect of living a life full of thanksgiving is an anxiety-free life full of peace and answered prayer. He stressed to the Philippians:

Be careful for nothing; but in every thing by prayer and supplication with thanksgiving let your requests be made known unto God. And the peace of God, which passeth all understanding, shall keep your hearts and minds through Christ Jesus. (Philippians 4:6-7)

I have been particularly blessed by a lesson I learned over 20 years ago. We were taught that whenever you are

NOW THAT YOU HAVE RECEIVED CHRIST

happy and thankful to God, the devil is sad, but whenever we are sad and ungrateful he is happy. Every wise child of God should therefore resolve to be happy and thankful, if only to deny the devil any success in his primary mission of killing, stealing and destroying (John 10:10).

It is my prayer that every reader of this book will grow in every area of grace that we have discussed and many more. I also pray that the devil will not succeed in stealing your joy in Jesus' name.

Chapter 7
Without me ye can do nothing

I am the vine, ye are the branches: He that abideth in me, and I in him, the same bringeth forth much fruit: for without me ye can do nothing (John 15:5)

Of great importance to our success in our Christian walk is the need to rely on Christ.

Very often, I hear mature Christians make reference to the period they accepted Christ and the testimonies that ensued. Many attest to the fact that they received answers to all their prayers and had a close fellowship with God. However as they grew older in the faith, answers to prayers took longer to arrive, and some of the same Christians do not now display as much zeal or have the same assurance of God's presence.

There is a school of thought that says God would do everything for baby Christians, just like human parents will. I am sure you know that when a child is born, the parents bathe the child, change its clothes and feed it. Every provision a child requires is met by the parents, but as a child grows older a level of responsibility is expected from him by the parents. In the same way, as we progress in our walk with God, He expects a level of maturity from us. This should not, however, affect our zeal for the things of God or the answers to our prayers.

The challenges for a lot of Christians arise because their dependability on God begins to wane as they grow in the faith. Many begin to develop self-confidence or rely solely on their good works, while totally abandoning God's grace. This is a very dangerous path to tread and must be totally avoided by anyone who wants to make progress in the Christian race.

In Paul's letter to the Galatians, a group of Jewish

Christians were required to become circumcised in order to authenticate their relationship with Christ. Paul the Apostle warned them against the danger of relying on works, as this will only amount to a fall from grace. He stressed:

Stand fast therefore in the liberty wherewith Christ hath made us free, and be not entangled again with the yoke of bondage. Behold, I Paul say unto you, that if ye be circumcised, that he is a debtor to do the whole law. Christ is become of no effect unto you, whosoever of you are justified by the law; ye are fallen from grace. (Galatians 5:1-4)

It is clear from Paul's statement above that seeking to please God through the deeds of the law and the abandonment of grace leads to bondage and alienation from Christ. The way forward therefore is to rely completely on Christ by maintaining a close fellowship with Him, drawing strength from Him and being obedient to Him. In order to fully understand how this can be achieved, we will look at another statement made by our Lord and Saviour Jesus as a follow up to our opening Scripture:

If ye abide in me, and my words abide in you, ye
shall ask what ye will, and it shall be done unto you.
(John 15:7)

It is clear from our opening Scripture that our success
as Christians is dependent on our total reliance on
Christ, but the following statement in verse 7 of John
chapter 15 explains the processes we must follow in
order to achieve such success. These processes and the
resultant effects are listed below and will be further
elaborated upon:

1. Abide in me
2. My words abide in you
3. You will ask what you will
4. It shall be done unto you – bring forth fruit

1. ABIDE IN ME

If we accept Jesus Christ as our Lord and Saviour but
then wander away from Him, or we return to our old
ways of living, we are not taking our faith seriously. If
someone enrols for a degree at a university and does
not stay for tuition or do any coursework or exams,
but leaves immediately after enrolment, such a person
should not expect to graduate or earn any degree at

the university. Salvation is only the beginning of our Christian journey; eternal life with God is our final destination. If after being saved we give up on the Christian life, we cannot be guaranteed eternal life. Therefore, we must abide in Christ.

What then does it mean to abide in Christ? The word 'abide', as used in the King James version, is equated with the word 'remain' in many of the other translations. This in effect means staying put, staying behind, staying on or hanging about. I particularly like the phrase "to hang about" as you are greatly influenced by the people you hang around with. This is because you play together, take counsel from one another, eat together and do a lot of other intimate things together, depending on the depth of your relationship.

Jesus Christ is calling on us as believers to hang out with Him, and for us to do this we must get to know Him, understand His likes and dislikes, follow Him to the places He hangs out in, and generally ensure that we maintain a solid relationship with Him.

The key to understanding how to fulfil Christ's instruction for us to abide in Him can be found in the ninth and tenth verses of John 15:

As the Father hath loved me, so have I loved you: continue
ye in my love. If ye keep my commandments, ye shall abide
in my love; even as I have kept my Father's commandments,
and abide in his love. (John 15:9-10)

1. **We must know Him enough to understand His likes
   and dislikes.** Through hanging out with Him we listen
   to His instructions and observe His lifestyle so that
   we can emulate Him.

2. **We must love Him enough to obey Him**. We take
   counsel from Him because we trust and reverence
   Him. Our trust in Him is based on our knowledge
   of His unfailing love for us, which we reciprocate by
   loving Him in return. We demonstrate our love for
   Him by our obedience to His commands.

2. MY WORDS ABIDE IN YOU

While we have already touched on the need to know and
understand the Word of God earlier in this book, it still
cannot be overemphasised – especially when many human
philosophies and motivational teachings are flaunted as
the Word of God. Jesus identified this problem during
His ministry here on earth and warned about its danger:

He was also saying to them, "You are experts at setting aside and nullifying the commandment of God in order to keep your [man-made] tradition and regulations. For Moses said, 'Honor your father and your mother [with respect and gratitude]'; and, 'He who speaks evil of his father or mother must be put to death'; but you [Pharisees and scribes] say, 'If a man tells his father or mother, "Whatever I have that would help you is Corban, (that is to say, already a gift to God),"' then you no longer let him do anything for his father or mother [since helping them would violate his vow of Corban]; so you nullify the [authority of the] word of God [acting as if it did not apply] because of your tradition which you have handed down [through the elders]. And you do many things such as that." (Mark 7:9-13, AMP).

If we want Christ's Word to abide in us we must be able to distinguish between His Word and the words of human philosophy. While some human philosophies may not be bad in themselves, they will not produce for us the same effect as Christ's teaching.

Taking the same phrase that I used in the last section, one can say that the Word of God should "hang out" with us. But this will only be possible if we create the right environment for the Word of God to 'hang out' in.

Our lives must become like the good soil that a farmer sows seed upon, as described by Jesus in the Parable of the Sower. If we hang out with His Word its effect is to make us so familiar with Him that we can easily distinguish His voice.

The Bible records:

> *And he spake many things unto them in parables, saying, Behold, a sower went forth to sow; and when he sowed, some seeds fell by the way side, and the fowls came and devoured them up: Some fell upon stony places, where they had not much earth: and forthwith they sprung up, because they had no deepness of earth: And when the sun was up, they were scorched; and because they had no root, they withered away. And some fell among thorns; and the thorns sprung up, and choked them: But other fell into good ground, and brought forth fruit, some an hundredfold, some sixtyfold, some thirtyfold.* (Matthew 13:3-8)

> *But he that received seed into the good ground is he that heareth the word, and understandeth it; which also beareth fruit, and bringeth forth, some an hundredfold, some sixty, some thirty.* (Matthew 13:23)

Jesus gave us a clear indication of what we must be in order to decipher His voice. We must become His sheep. He taught:

> *But he that entereth in by the door is the shepherd of the sheep. To him the porter openeth; and the sheep hear his voice: and he calleth his own sheep by name, and leadeth them out. And when he putteth forth his own sheep, he goeth before them, and the sheep follow him: for they know his voice. And a stranger will they not follow, but will flee from him: for they know not the voice of strangers.* (John 10:2-5)

> *But ye believe not, because ye are not of my sheep, as I said unto you. My sheep hear my voice, and I know them, and they follow me: And I give unto them eternal life; and they shall never perish, neither shall any man pluck them out of my hand. My Father, which gave them me, is greater than all; and no man is able to pluck them out of my Father's hand.* (John 10:26-29)

I pray that every reader of this book who has accepted Jesus as their Lord and Saviour will stay in close proximity to His word through study and meditation, to the extent that they will become His sheep, recognising His voice and fleeing from the stranger.

3. YOU WILL ASK WHAT YOU WILL

Another issue that we have dealt with and shall be touching upon again is prayer. It is often said that "prayer is the master key", and it doesn't matter how bad or difficult one's problem might be, it we take it to God in prayer, He will provide a solution.

In the context of John 10:7, prayer results from an intimate relationship with Christ and His Word. The product of such a relationship is a life that is holy and Christ-like, and the prayers that flow from such a person will be heartfelt, sincere and unselfish. God always listens to such kinds of prayer:

And this is the confidence that we have in him, that, if we ask any thing according to his will, he heareth us: And if we know that he hear us, whatsoever we ask, we know that we have the petitions that we desired of him. (1 John 5:14-15)

We can only hold on to a confidence that God

will hear and answer us when we ask according to His will. Unfortunately, a lot of Christians today are deceived into saying prayers that are selfish or outright evil, and they expect God to answer. Some pray for their enemies to die, and these so-called enemies could even be fellow believers who may have offended them! If we have truly hung out with Christ and imbibed His Word, we will know that He advocates forgiveness and requires us to be positive in our outlook on life.

While it is true that we can ask God for anything we want, this must be done in love and in line with our Master's will. It is crucial to note from the scripture below that this unselfish style of prayer is expected from us as children of God.

Ye have heard that it hath been said, Thou shalt love thy neighbour, and hate thine enemy. But I say unto you, Love your enemies, bless them that curse you, do good to them that hate you, and pray for them which despitefully use you, and persecute you; that ye may be the children of your Father which is in heaven: for he maketh his sun to rise on the evil and on the good, and sendeth rain on the just and on the unjust. For if ye love them which love you, what reward have ye? Do not even the publicans the same? And if ye salute your brethren only, what do ye more than others? Do not even the publicans so? Be ye therefore perfect, even as your Father which is in heaven is perfect. (Matthew 5:43-48)

4. IT SHALL BE DONE UNTO YOU – BRING FORTH FRUIT

Throughout the Bible, we note that God takes pleasure in listening to the prayers of His people and granting their requests. I have linked this with fruitfulness because our relationship with Christ and His Word should lead us to offer prayers that produce fruitful results. We are encouraged by the Psalmist to commit all our business to God, having confidence that He will prosper us.

Delight thyself also in the LORD: and he shall give thee the desires of thine heart. Commit thy way unto the LORD; trust also in him; and he shall bring it to pass. And he shall bring forth thy righteousness as the light, and thy judgment as the noonday. (Psalm 37:4-6)

I particularly love what Jesus said about the requests we make (prayer) when He addressed His disciples in John 16, as it demonstrates to us how He takes pleasure in seeing us fulfilled. His desire is to give us fullness of joy.

Hitherto have ye asked nothing in my name: ask, and ye shall receive, that your joy may be full. (John 16:24)

I pray for every reader of this book, that as you walk with Jesus in your journey of faith, He will make you fruitful and that you will have an amazing relationship with Him. As you present your requests to Him, He will answer you and your joy will be full, in Jesus' name. Amen.

Useful tips for new believers

In the introduction of this book, I mentioned that I was fortunate to receive good counsel and follow-up from people who had been on the Christian journey before me. I have highlighted below a few ideas that a new believer can take on in order to ensure growth. Please note that these tips are not exhaustive and feel free to follow the guidance of the Holy Spirit, who now resides in you and will guide you in the right direction (John 14:26; Romans 8:14)

1. **Ha**ve a regular time for the study of God's **Word.** This is essential food for your spirit and helps to ensure growth. See 1 Peter 2:2; 1 Timothy 4:15; 2 Timothy 2:15. Alongside studying, I remember being advised

by a brother to write out a verse of the Bible each day and take it with me wherever I went, with the aim of memorising it. Memorising the scriptures can be very helpful in our growth as new believers as it helps us to know God's counsel, which we can apply for use in our lifestyle and prayers.

2. **Develop a solid faith in God.** This follows on from having a regular time of study because faith is developed through a knowledge of the personality of God, and this knowledge can only come through an understanding of His Word (Romans 10:17 – "*So then faith cometh by hearing, and hearing by the word of God*"). The recommended way for a believer to live according to the Bible is by faith (Romans 1:17; Galatians 3:11). Faith is also an essential requirement that a believer needs in order to please God (Hebrews 11:6 – "*But without faith it is impossible to please him: for he that cometh to God must believe that he is, and that he is a rewarder of them that diligently seek him*").

3. **Have a regular time for prayer**. Prayer affords us the opportunity to fellowship with God and should be done at every opportunity (1 Thessalonians 5:17), but we should also set aside time when we consistently fellowship with Him in prayer. Some refer to this period as a "quiet time", not because you

are silent but during this time, apart from making your requests known to God, you can reflect on His Word and wait on Him to speak back to you. Jesus engaged in this kind of practice, as can be seen in Mark 1:35, for example.

4. Have regular fellowship with other Christians. Identify and get connected to a congregation where God is being worshipped in spirit and in truth. When we receive Jesus Christ as our Lord and Saviour, we become born again into the Body of Christ, that is, the Church. Within the Body, we can identify our specific role, and as we perform our responsibility within the Body we grow up in the faith (Hebrews 10:24–25; 1 Corinthians 12:27-28).

5. Use every opportunity you have to witness about Christ. The earlier we start to share our faith with others the better for us. One major reason God did not take us away from this world after He saved us is because He wants us to represent Him in the ministry of reconciliation (reconciling people with God – 2 Corinthians 5:17-20). I'd like to mention the need to do this lovingly. If indeed God has been good to us we should be ready to share His goodness with others (2 Timothy 4:2). We must do this in line with God's will and using God's method. A verse of the Bible that I love so much is John 3:17: "*For God*

NOW THAT YOU HAVE RECEIVED CHRIST

sent not his son into the world to condemn the world; but that the world through him might be saved." We should ensure that our message is indeed one of good news and not a message of condemnation. Prior to giving our lives to Christ, some of us had a lot of people present the gospel to us but we did not accept the message because their method was off-putting. We should therefore guard against using the same methods we did not like when we preach the gospel to others.

6. **Be prepared for opposition.** During many evangelistic programmes, people are told that once they accept Jesus Christ as their Lord and Saviour, all their problems are over. This may not be entirely true, as our stand for Christ opens us up for opposition from Satan, the world and even some who profess to be believers. However, we should not be afraid or discouraged by this because God has already overcome the devil and the world for us. We only need to stand firm in our faith and resist the devil (Mathew 5:10-12; John 16:33; 1 Peter 5:8-10).

7. **Always be thankful.** With the knowledge that *"God causes everything to work together for the good of those who love God and are called according to his purpose for them"* (Romans 8:28, NLT), we should be thankful in every situation we find

ourselves because God will surely work out the situation in our favour. It might not seem so initially, but if we persevere in our gratitude to God, we will surely overcome (1 Thessalonians 5: 18; Colossians 2:7; Colossians 4:2).